3 CHORD SONGS
FOR
Mandolin

ISBN: 978-1-5400-0570-0

7777 W. BLUEMOUND RD. P.O. BOX 13819 MILWAUKEE, WI 53213

Visit Hal Leonard Online at
www.halleonard.com

MANDOLIN NOTATION LEGEND

Mandolin music can be notated three different ways: on a *musical staff*, in *tablature*, and in *rhythm slashes*.

RHYTHM SLASHES are written above the staff. Strum chords in the rhythm indicated. Use the chord diagrams found at the top of the first page of the transcription for the appropriate chord voicings.

THE MUSICAL STAFF shows pitches and rhythms and is divided by bar lines into measures. Pitches are named after the first seven letters of the alphabet.

TABLATURE graphically represents the mandolin fretboard. Each of the four horizontal lines represents each of the four courses of strings, and each number represents a fret.

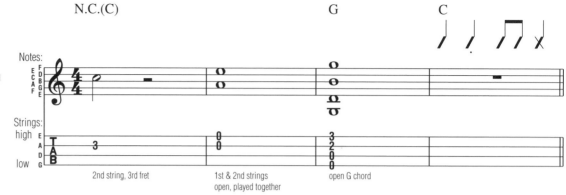

2nd string, 3rd fret   1st & 2nd strings open, played together   open G chord

Definitions for Special Mandolin Notation

MUTED STRING(S): Lightly touch a string with the edge of your fret-hand finger while fretting a note on an adjacent string, causing the muted string to be unheard. Muting all of the strings with the fingers of the fret-hand while strumming the strings with the picking hand produces a percussive effect.

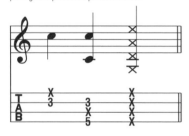

HAMMER-ON: Strike the first (lower) note with one finger, then sound the higher note (on the same string) with another finger by fretting it without picking.

PULL-OFF: Place both fingers on the notes to be sounded. Strike the first note and, without picking, pull the finger off to sound the second (lower) note.

LEGATO SLIDE: Strike the first note and then slide the same fret-hand finger up or down to the second note. The second note is not struck.

SHIFT SLIDE: Same as the legato slide except the second note is struck.

HALF-STEP BEND: Strike the note and bend up ½ step.

GRACE NOTE BEND: Strike the note and immediately bend up as indicated.

TREMOLO PICKING: The note is picked rapidly and continuously.

Additional Musical Definitions

p *(piano)* — • Play quietly.

mp *(mezzo-piano)* — • Play moderately quiet.

mf *(mezzo-forte)* — • Play moderately loud.

f *(forte)* — • Play loudly.

cont. rhy. sim. — • Continue strumming in similar rhythm.

N.C. *(no chord)* — • Don't strum until the next chord symbol. Chord symbols in parentheses reflect implied harmony.

D.S. al Coda — • Go back to the sign (𝄋), then play until the measure marked *"To Coda"*, then skip to the section labeled *"Coda."*

D.S.S. al Coda 2 — • Go back to the double sign (𝄋𝄋), then play until the measure marked *"To Coda 2"*, then skip to the section labeled *"Coda 2."*

D.S. al Fine — • Go back to the sign (𝄋), then play until the label *"Fine."*

(staccato) — • Play the note or chord short.

rit. *(ritard)* — • Gradually slow down.

(fermata) — • Hold the note or chord for an undetermined amount of time.

• Repeat measures between signs.

1. **2.** — • When a repeated section has different endings, play the first ending only the first time and the second ending only the second time.

NOTE: Tablature numbers in parentheses mean:
1. The note is being sustained over a system (note in standard notation is tied), or
2. The note is sustained, but a new articulation (such as a hammer-on, pull-off or slide) begins.

Ain't No Sunshine

Words and Music by Bill Withers

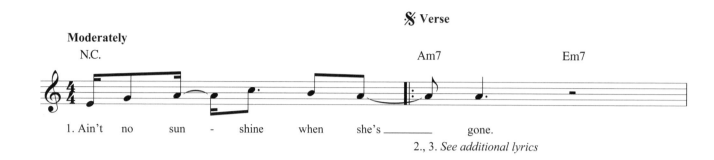

%. **Verse**

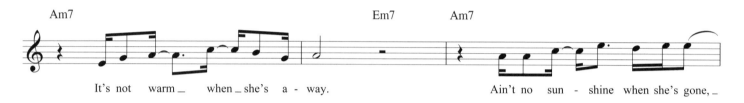

1. Ain't no sun - shine when she's _____ gone.
2., 3. *See additional lyrics*

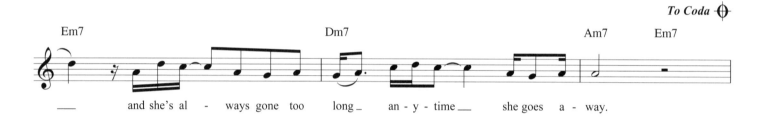

It's not warm _ when _ she's a - way. Ain't no sun - shine when she's gone, _

To Coda ⊕

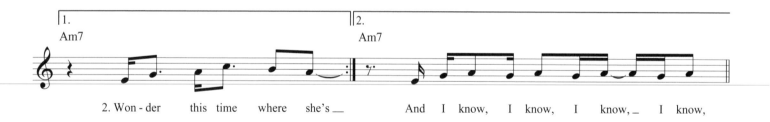

_ and she's al - ways gone too long _ an - y - time _ she goes a - way.

2. Won - der this time where she's _ And I know, I know, I know, _ I know,

Bridge

I know, I know, I know, _ I know, _ I know, I know, I know, _ I know, _ I know, I know, I know, _

_ I know, I know, I know, I know, _ I know, I know, I know, I know, _ I know, I know, I

know, hey, __ I ought to leave the young thing a - lone, ___ but ain't no sun - shine when she's _

D.S. al Coda

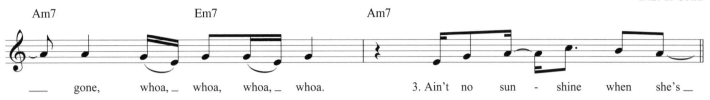

Am7   Em7   Am7

__ gone, whoa, _ whoa, whoa, _ whoa.   3. Ain't no sun - shine when she's __

✿ Coda

Am7   Em7   Am7

Play 3 times

An - y - time _ she goes a - way.

Additional Lyrics

2. Wonder this time where she's gone,
   Wonder if she's gone to stay.
   Ain't no sunshine when she's gone,
   And this house just ain't no home
   Anytime she goes away.

3. Ain't no sunshine when she's gone,
   Only darkness everyday.
   Ain't no sunshine when she's gone,
   And this house just ain't no home
   Anytime she goes away.

All About That Bass

Words and Music by Kevin Kadish and Meghan Trainor

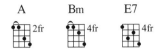

Chorus
Moderately fast

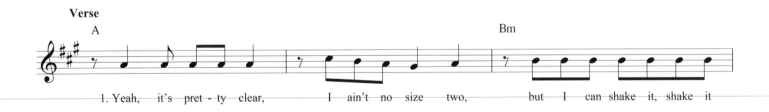

work - in' that Pho - to - shop. We know that sh** ain't real, come on now, make it stop.

If you got beau - ty, beau - ty, just raise 'em up, 'cause ev - 'ry inch of you is per - fect from the

Pre-Chorus

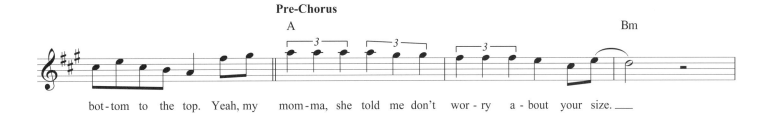

bot - tom to the top. Yeah, my mom - ma, she told me don't wor - ry a - bout your size. ___

She says, "Boys like a lit - tle more boot - y to hold at night." ___

You know I won't be no stick fig - ure, sil - i - cone Bar - bie doll. ___

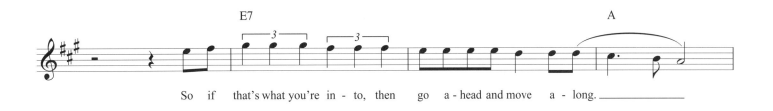

So if that's what you're in - to, then go a - head and move a - long. ___

Chorus

Be - cause you know I'm all a - bout that bass, 'bout that bass, no tre - ble. I'm

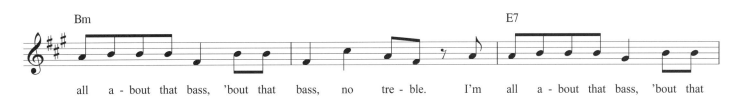

all a - bout that bass, 'bout that bass, no tre - ble. I'm all a - bout that bass, 'bout that

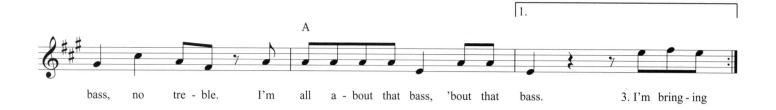

bass, no tre - ble. I'm all a - bout that bass, 'bout that bass. 3. I'm bring - ing

Outro

A

bass. Be - cause you know I'm all a - bout that bass, 'bout that bass, no tre - ble. I'm

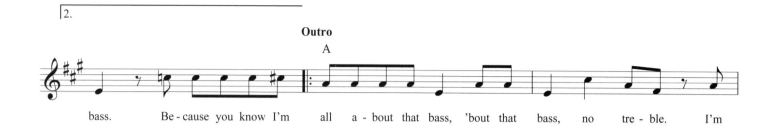

Bm   E7

all a - bout that bass, 'bout that bass, no tre - ble. I'm all a - bout that bass, 'bout that

Repeat and fade

A

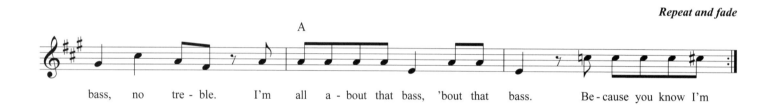

bass, no tre - ble. I'm all a - bout that bass, 'bout that bass. Be - cause you know I'm

Additional Lyrics

3. I'm bringing booty back.
   Go ahead and tell them skinny bitches that.
   Nah, I'm just playin'. I know you think you're fat,
   But I'm here to tell you
   Every inch of you is perfect from the bottom to the top.

All Along the Watchtower

Words and Music by Bob Dylan

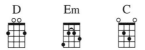

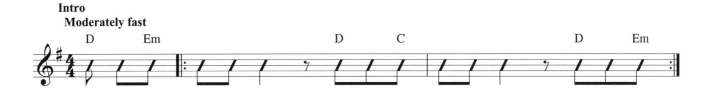

Intro
Moderately fast

Verse

1. "There must be some kind of way out of here," said the jok-er to the thief. ___
2., 3. *See additional lyrics*

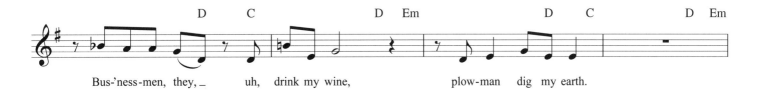

"There's too much con-fu-sion, I can't get no re-lief. ___

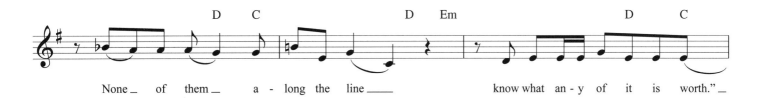

Bus-'ness-men, they, ___ uh, drink my wine, plow-man dig my earth.

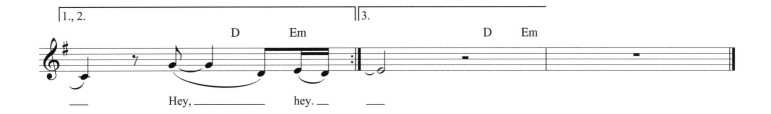

None ___ of them ___ a-long the line ___ know what an-y of it is worth." ___

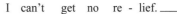

|1., 2. |3.

Hey, _____ hey. ___ ___

Additional Lyrics

2. "No reason to get excited," the thief, he kindly spoke.
   "There are many here among us who feel that life is but a joke,
   But you and I, we've been through that, and this is not our fate.
   So, let us not talk falsely now, the hour's getting late."

3. All along the watchtower, princes kept the view,
   While all the women came and went, barefoot servants, too.
   Well, outside in the cold distance, a wildcat did growl.
   Two riders were approaching and the wind began to howl.

Blue Eyes Crying in the Rain

Words and Music by Fred Rose

Cold, Cold Heart

Words and Music by Hank Williams

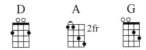

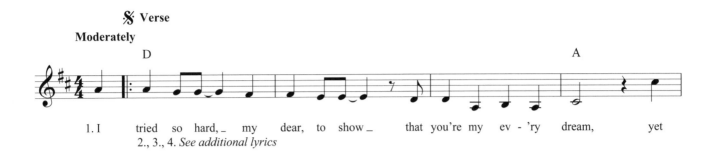

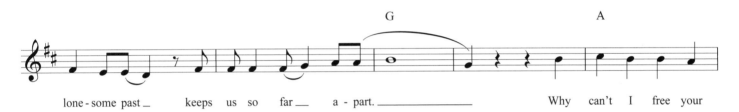

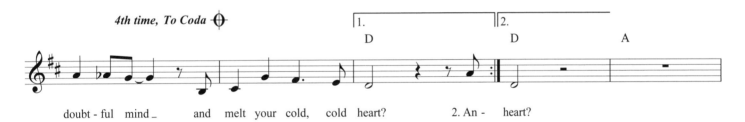

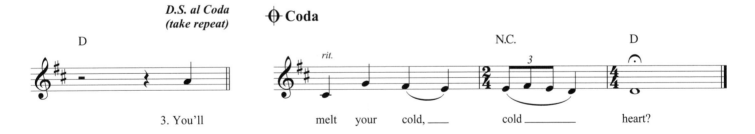

Additional Lyrics

2. Another love before my time made your heart sad and blue.
And so my heart is paying now for things I didn't do.
In anger unkind words are said that make the teardrops start.
Why can't I free your doubtful mind, and melt your cold, cold heart?

3. You'll never know how much it hurts to see you sit and cry.
You know you need and want my love, yet you're afraid to try.
Why do you run and hide from life? To try it just ain't smart.
Why can't I free your doubtful mind and melt your cold, cold heart?

4. There was a time when I believed that you belonged to me.
But, now I know your heart is shackled to a memory.
The more I learn to care for you, the more we drift apart.
Why can't I free your doubtful mind and melt your cold, cold heart?

Blue Suede Shoes

Words and Music by Carl Lee Perkins

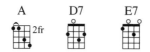

A   D7   E7

% Verse

Moderately fast

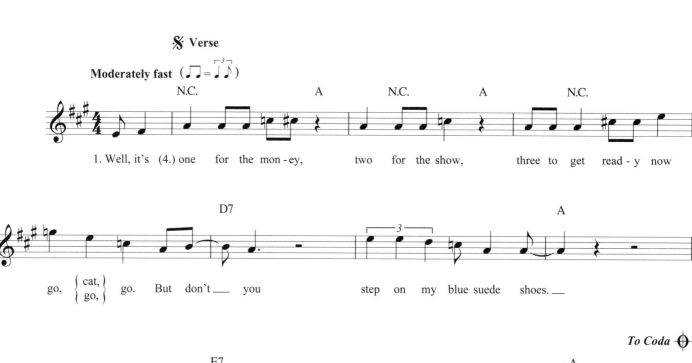

1. Well, it's (4.) one for the mon-ey, two for the show, three to get read-y now

go, { cat, go, } go. But don't ___ you step on my blue suede shoes. ___

To Coda

Well, you can do an-y-thing but lay off ___ of my blue suede shoes.

Verse

2. Well, you can knock me down, ___ step in my face, ___
burn my house, ___ steal ___ my car, ___

slan-der my name all ___ o-ver the place. }
drink ___ my liq-uor from an old ___ fruit jar. }
And do an-y-thing ___ that you

wan-na do, ___ but uh, uh, hon-ey, lay off ___ of { my them } shoes. And don't ___ you

step on my blue suede shoes.

You can do an-y-thing but lay off _

1. _ of my blue suede shoes.

D.S. al Coda

3. Well, you can

4. Well, it's a

⊕ Coda

Outro

Well, it's blue, blue, blue suede shoes.

Blue, blue, blue suede shoes, yeah. Blue, blue, blue suede shoes, ba - by.

Blue, blue, blue suede shoes. You can do an - y - thing _ but lay off _

_ of my blue suede shoes.

Bye Bye Love

Words and Music by Felice Bryant and Boudleaux Bryant

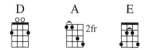

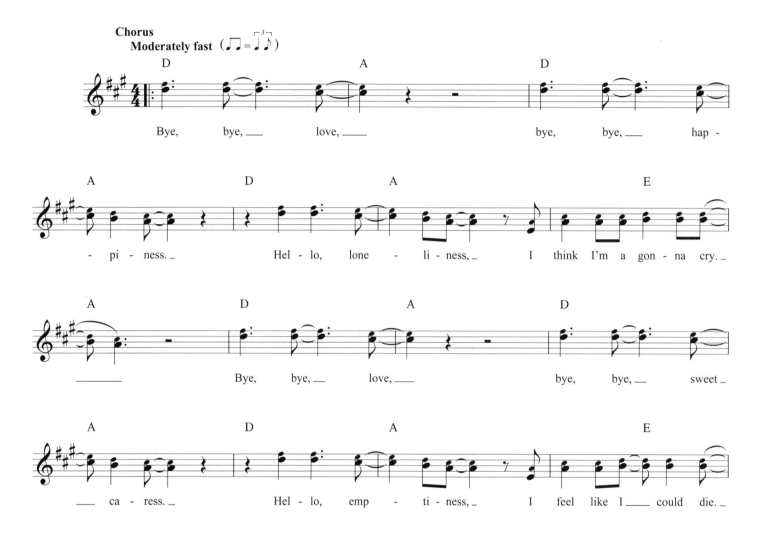

hap - py, _____ I sure am blue. She was my
count - in' _____ the stars a - bove. And here's the

ba - by _____ 'til he _____ stepped in. _____ Good - bye to _____
rea - son _____ that I'm _____ so free, _____ my lov - in' _____

2nd time, D.C. al Coda

ro - mance _____ that might have been. _____
ba - by _____ is through with me. _____

Coda

Outro   *Repeat and fade*

_____ Bye, bye, _____ my love, _ good - bye, _____ Bye, bye, _

Cecilia

Words and Music by Paul Simon

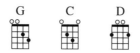

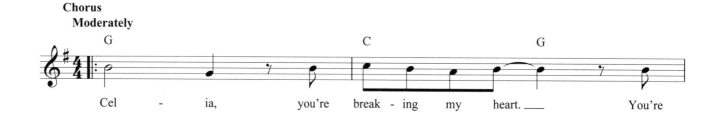

Coda

_____ Come on home. _____ Oh, oh,

Bridge

oh, oh, _____ oh, oh, oh, oh, oh, oh, oh, oh, _____ oh. _____ Ju - bi -

Outro

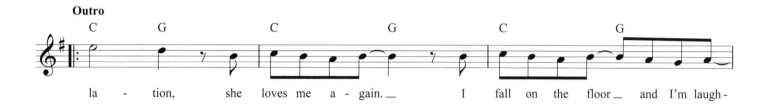

la - tion, she loves me a - gain. _____ I fall on the floor _____ and I'm laugh-

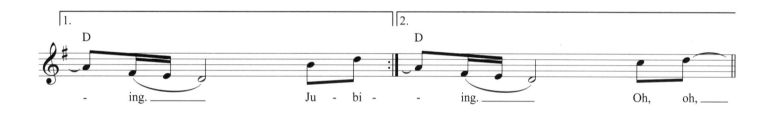

1.
\- ing. _____ Ju - bi -

2.
\- ing. _____ Oh, oh, _____

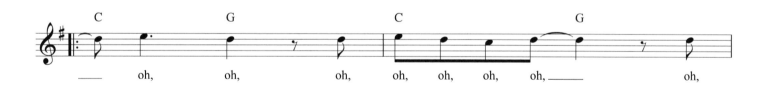

_____ oh, oh, oh, oh, oh, oh, oh, _____ oh,

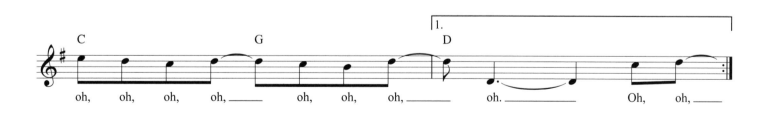

oh, oh, oh, oh, _____ oh, oh, oh, _____ oh.

1.
Oh, oh, _____

2.

_____ oh. Come on home. _____

Down on the Corner

Words and Music by John Fogerty

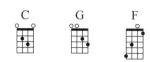

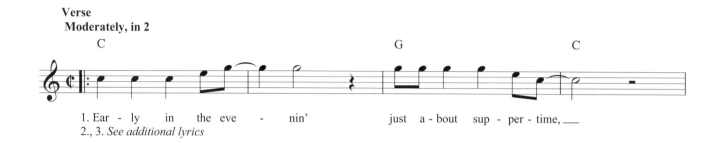

Verse
Moderately, in 2

1. Ear - ly in the eve - nin' just a - bout sup - per - time, ___
2., 3. *See additional lyrics*

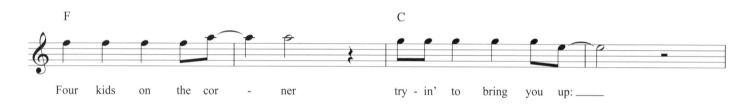

o - ver by the court - house they're start - in' to un - wind.

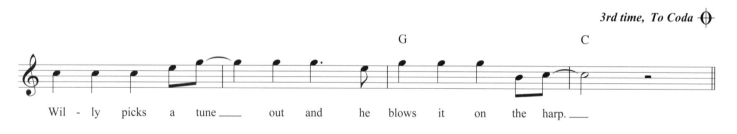

Four kids on the cor - ner try - in' to bring you up: ___

3rd time, To Coda ⊕

Wil - ly picks a tune ___ out and he blows it on the harp. ___

Chorus

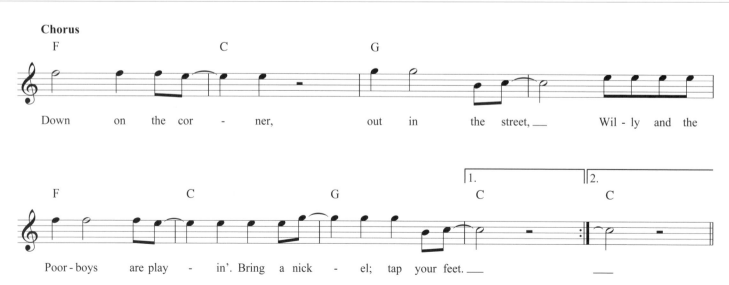

Down on the cor - ner, out in the street, ___ Wil - ly and the

Poor - boys are play - in'. Bring a nick - el; tap your feet. ___

Interlude

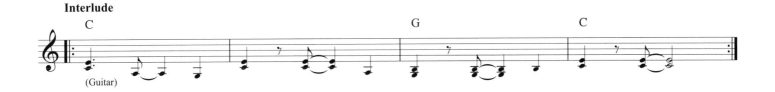

D.C. al Coda

⊕ Coda

Outro-Chorus

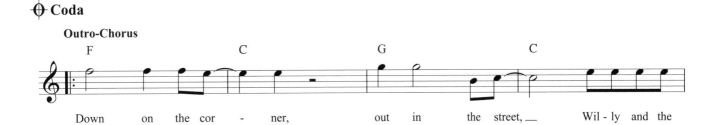

Down   on   the   cor   -   ner,   out   in   the   street, __   Wil - ly   and   the

Repeat and fade

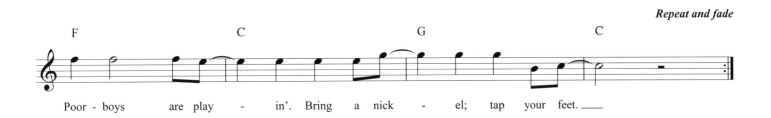

Poor - boys   are   play   -   in'.   Bring   a   nick   -   el;   tap   your   feet. ___

Additional Lyrics

2. Rooster hits the washboard, people just gotta smile.
    Blinky thumbs the guts bass and solos for a while.
    Poorboy twangs the rhythm out on his Kalamazoo.
    Willy goes into a dance and doubles on kazoo.

3. You don't need a penny just to hand around.
    But if you've got a nickel, won't you lay your money down?
    Over on the corner there's a happy noise.
    People come from all around to watch the magic boy.

Eleanor Rigby

Words and Music by John Lennon and Paul McCartney

Additional Lyrics

2. Father McKenzie,
   Writing the words of a sermon that no one will hear,
   No one comes near.
   Look at him working,
   Darning his socks in the night when there's nobody there.
   What does he dare?

3. Eleanor Rigby
   Died in the church and was buried along with her name,
   Nobody came.
   Father McKenzie,
   Wiping the dirt from his hands as he walks from the grave.
   No one was saved.

Folsom Prison Blues

Words and Music by John R. Cash

Additional Lyrics

2. When I was just a baby, my mama told me, "Son,
   Always be a good boy, don't ever play with guns."
   But I show a man in Reno just to watch him die.
   When I hear that whistle blowin', I hang my head and cry.

3. I bet there's rich folks eatin' in a fancy dining car.
   They're probably drinkin' coffee and smokin' big cigars.
   Well, I know I had it comin', I know I can't be free.
   But those people keep a movin' that's what tortures me.

4. Well, if they freed me from this prison, if that railroad train was mine.
   I bet I'd move it on a little farther down the line,
   Far from Folsom Prison, that's where I long to say.
   And then I'd let that lonesome whistle blow my blues away.

The First Cut Is the Deepest

Words and Music by Cat Stevens

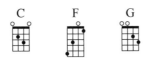

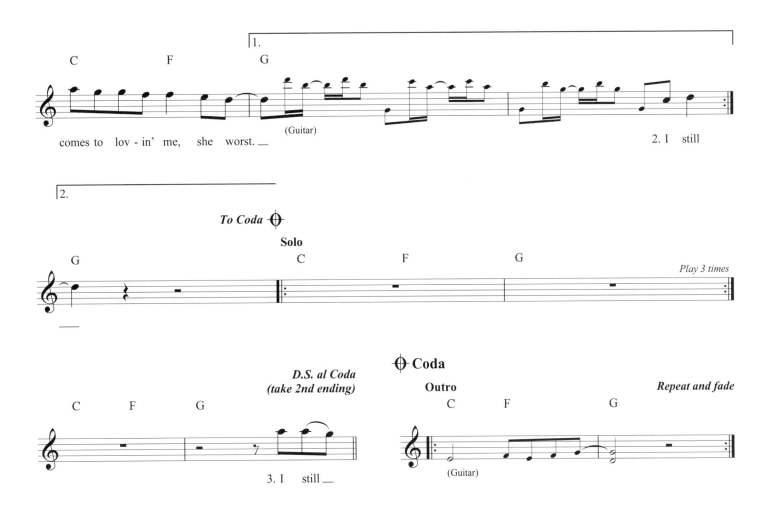

comes to lov-in' me, she worst. ___ (Guitar) 2. I still

Additional Lyrics

2. I still want you by my side,
   Just to help me dry the tears that I've cried.
   And I'm sure gonna give you a try.
   But, if you want, I'll try to love again.
   Baby, I'll try to love again but I know...

3. I still want you by my side,
   Just to help me dry the tears that I've cried.
   And I'm sure gonna give you a try.
   'Cause, if you want, I'll try to love again.
   Baby, I'll try to love again but I know...

For What It's Worth

Words and Music by Stephen Stills

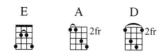

Verse
Moderately

1. There's some-thing hap-pen-ing here, ___ but what it is ain't ex-act-ly clear. ___
2., 3., 4. *See additional lyrics*

___ There's a man with a gun o-ver there ___ tell-ing

me I've got to be-ware. ___ I think it's time we stop, chil-dren; what's that sound? ___

1., 2., 3.

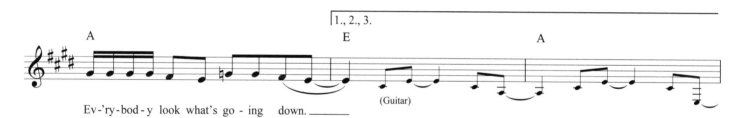

Ev-'ry-bod-y look what's go-ing down. ___ (Guitar)

4.

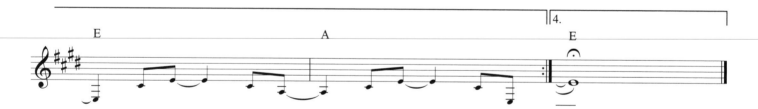

Additional Lyrics

2. There's battle lines being drawn.
   Nobody's right if everybody's wrong.
   Young people speaking their minds,
   Getting so much resistance from behind.
   I think it's time we stop; hey, what's that sound?
   Everybody look what's going down.

3. What a field day for the heat.
   A thousand people in the street,
   Singing songs and carrying signs,
   Mostly say, "Hooray for our side."
   It's time we stop; hey, what's that sound?
   Everybody look what's going down.

4. Paranoia strikes deep,
   Into your life it will creep.
   It starts when you're always afraid.
   Step out of line, the man come and take you away.
   We better stop; hey, what's that sound?
   Everybody look what's going down.

Louie, Louie

Words and Music by Richard Berry

Copyright © 1957 EMI Longitude Music
Copyright Renewed
All Rights Administered by Sony/ATV Music Publishing LLC, 424 Church Street, Suite 1200, Nashville, TN 37219
International Copyright Secured   All Rights Reserved

I Still Haven't Found What I'm Looking For

Words and Music by U2

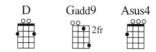

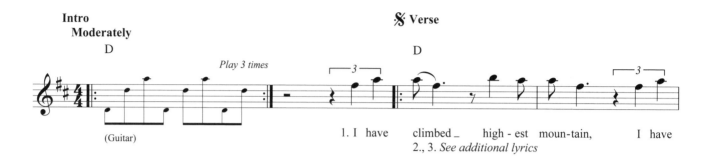

run ___ through the fields on - ly to be with ___ you, _____ on - ly to

be with ___ you. _____ I have run, ___ I have crawled, I have

scaled ___ these cit - y walls, _____ these cit - y walls, _____ on - ly to

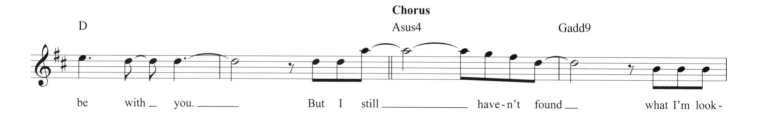

be with ___ you. _____ But I still _____ have-n't found ___ what I'm look-

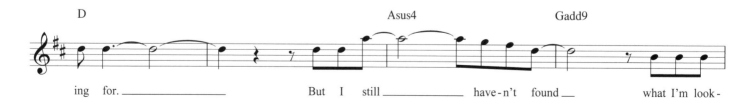

ing for. _____ But I still _____ have-n't found ___ what I'm look-

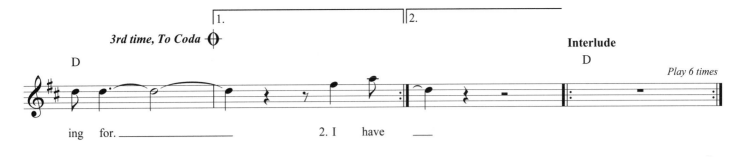

3rd time, To Coda ✛

Interlude

Play 6 times

ing for. _____ 2. I have ___

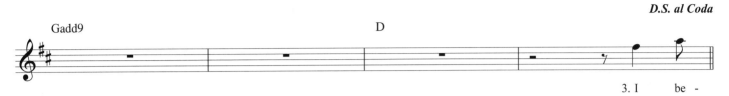

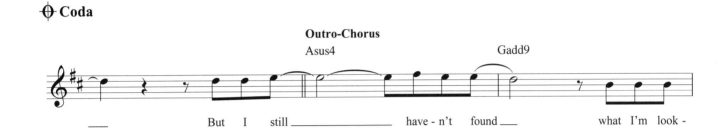

D.S. al Coda

3. I be -

✛ **Coda**

Outro-Chorus

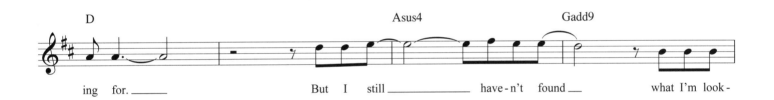

___ But I still _____ have-n't found ___ what I'm look -

Repeat and fade

ing for. _____ But I still _____ have-n't found ___ what I'm look -

ing for. _____

Additional Lyrics

2. I have kissed honey lips, felt the healing in her fingertips.
   It burned like fire, this burning desire.
   I have spoke with the tongue of angels, I have held the hand of a devil,
   It was warm in the night, I was cold as a stone.

3. I believe in the kingdom come, then all the colors will bleed into one,
   Bleed into one. But, yes, I'm still runnin'.
   You broke the bonds and you loosed the chains, carried the cross of my shame,
   Of my shame. You know I believe it.

The Joker

Words and Music by Steve Miller, Eddie Curtis and Ahmet Ertegun

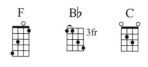

Jolene

Words and Music by Dolly Parton

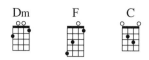

Intro
Moderately fast

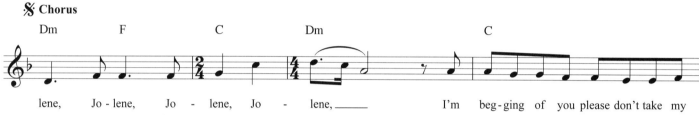

(Guitar)

Jo -

Chorus

lene,   Jo - lene,   Jo - lene,   Jo - lene, _____   I'm   beg-ging   of   you   please   don't   take   my

man.   Jo - lene,   Jo - lene,   Jo - lene,   Jo -

lene, _____   please   don't   take   him   just   be-cause   you   can.   1. Your

Verse

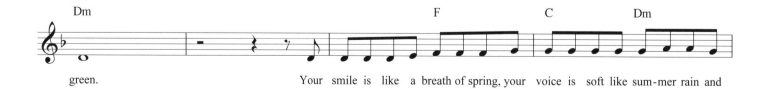

beau-ty   is   be-yond   com-pare   with   flam-ing   locks   of   au-burn   hair, with   i - v'ry   skin   and   eyes   of   em-'rald
2., 3., See additional lyrics

green.   Your   smile   is   like   a   breath   of   spring,   your   voice   is   soft   like   sum-mer   rain   and

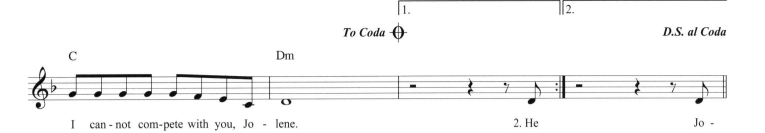

To Coda ⊕   *D.S. al Coda*

C   Dm

I can-not com-pete with you, Jo - lene.   2. He   Jo -

⊕ **Coda**

Chorus
Dm   F   C   Dm

Jo - lene,   Jo - lene,   Jo - lene,   Jo - lene,_____   I'm

C   Dm   F

beg - gin' of you please don't take my   man.   Jo - lene,   Jo - lene,   Jo -

C   Dm   C   Dm

lene,   Jo - lene,_____   please don't take him e - ven through you   can._____

Jo - lene,   Jo - lene._____

Outro   *Repeat and fade*

(Guitar)

Additional Lyrics

2. He talks about you in his sleep
   And there's nothing I can do to keep
   From crying when he calls your name, Jolene.
   And I can easily understand
   How you could easily take my man
   But you don't know what he means to me, Jolene.

3. You could have your choice of men
   But I could never love again.
   He's the only one for me, Jolene.
   I had to have this talk with you.
   My happiness depends on you
   And whatever you decide to do, Jolene.

Lay Down Sally

Words and Music by Eric Clapton, Marcy Levy and George Terry

Don't you think_ you want_ some - one _ to talk _ to?

Lay down, Sal - ly, no need to leave _ so soon. _

3rd time, To Coda ⊕

I've been try - ing all _ night long _ just to

2nd time, D.S. al Coda

talk to you. _

2. The
3. I

⊕ **Coda**

Outro

w/ Intro riff

Repeat and fade

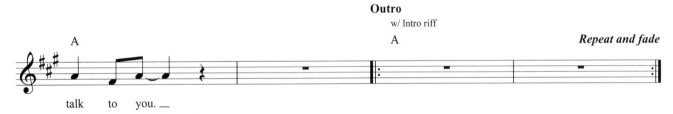

talk to you. _

Additional Lyrics

2. The sun ain't nearly on the rise,
   And we still got the moon and stars above.
   Underneath the velvet skies,
   Love is all that matters; won't you stay with me?
   And don't you ever leave.

3. I long to see the morning light
   Coloring your face so dreamily.
   So don't you go and say goodbye;
   You can lay your worries down and stay with me,
   And don't you ever leave.

Lean on Me

Words and Music by Bill Withers

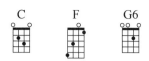

Verse
Moderately slow

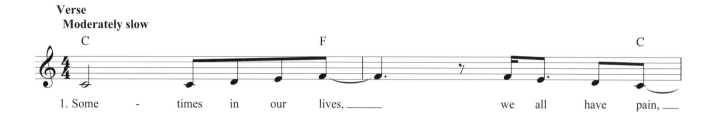

1. Some - times in our lives, _____ we all have pain, _____ we all have sor - rows. _____ But if we are wise, _____

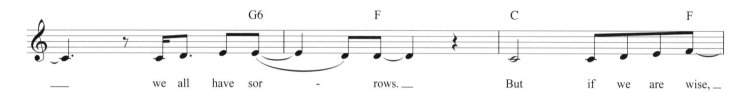

_____ we know that there's _____ al - ways to - mor - row. _____ Lean on me _____

𝄋 Chorus

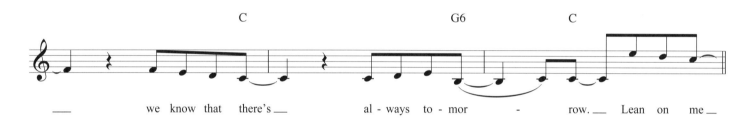

_____ when you're not strong, _____ and I'll be your friend, _____ I'll help you car -

- ry _____ on; _____ for it won't be long _____ 'til I'm gon - na need _____

Verse

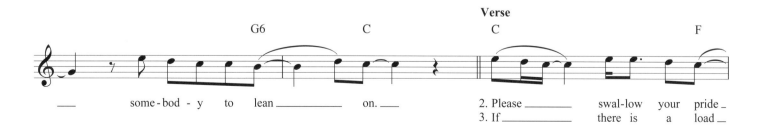

_____ some - bod - y to lean _____ on. _____ 2. Please _____ swal - low your pride _____
                                                       3. If _____ there is a load _____

if I have things ___ you need to bor - row. ___
you have to bear ___ that you can't car - ry. ___

To Coda

For no one can fill ___ those of your needs ___ that you won't let ___
I'm right up the road. ___ I'll share your load ___ if you just call ___

Bridge

___ show. _ You just call on me, broth - er, when you need a hand. _ We all ___

need some - bod - y to lean ___ on. ___ I just might have a prob - lem that

D.S. al Coda

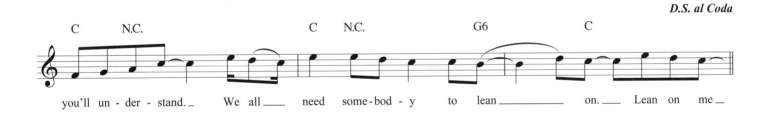

you'll un - der - stand. _ We all ___ need some - bod - y to lean ___ on. ___ Lean on me ___

Coda

Outro

Repeat and fade

___ me. ___ (Call ___ me, ___ call ___ me.) ___

Leaving on a Jet Plane

Words and Music by John Denver

hold   me   like ___ you'll   nev - er   let   me   go. _____   'Cause I'm

Chorus

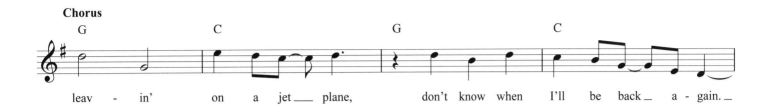
leav - in'   on   a   jet ___ plane,   don't know when   I'll   be   back ___ a - gain. ___

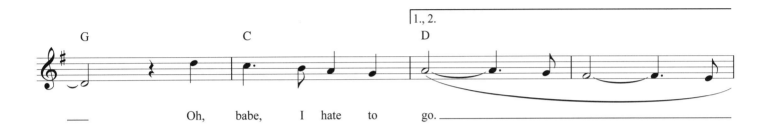
|1., 2.
___   Oh,   babe,   I   hate   to   go. _____

|3.
_____   2. There's so   go. _____   I'm

Outro-Chorus

leav - in'   on   a   jet ___ plane,   don't know when   I'll   be   back ___ a - gain. ___

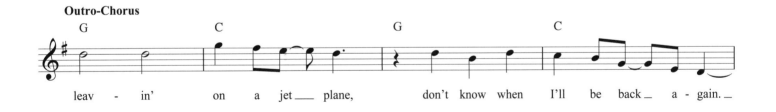
___   Oh,   babe, _____   I   hate   to   go. _____

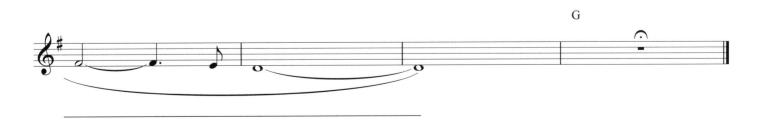

Love Me Do

Words and Music by John Lennon and Paul McCartney

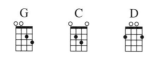

(Harmonica)

1.-4. Love, love me do, _____ you know I love you. _____ I'll

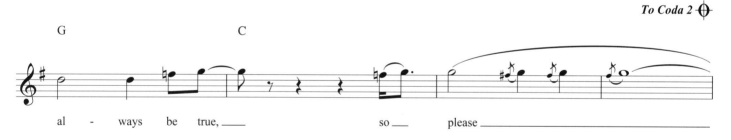

al - ways be true, _____ so _____ please _____

_____ love me do. _____ Whoa, _ love _____ me do. _____

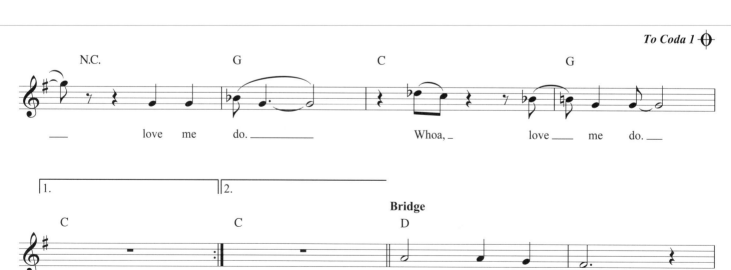

Some - one to love,

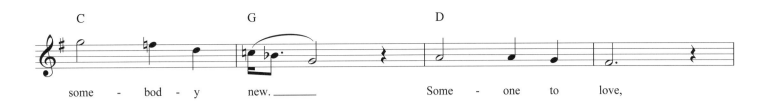

some - bod - y   new. _____   Some - one   to   love,

⊕ Coda 1

D.S. al Coda 1   **Harmonica Solo**

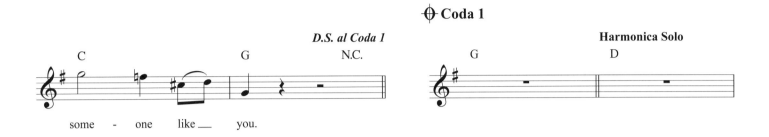

some - one   like __ you.

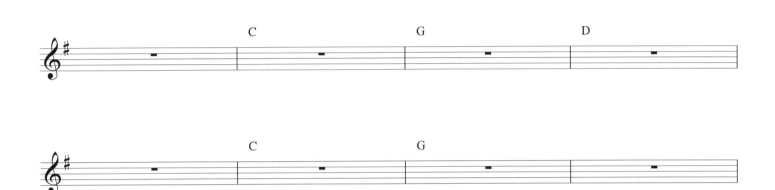

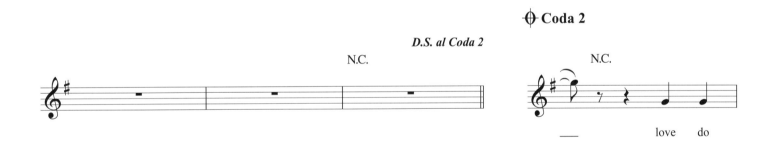

⊕ Coda 2

D.S. al Coda 2

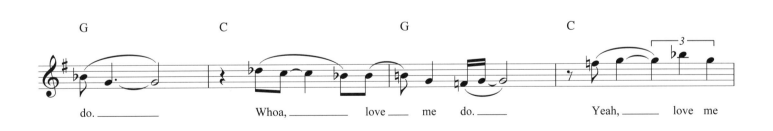

___   love   do

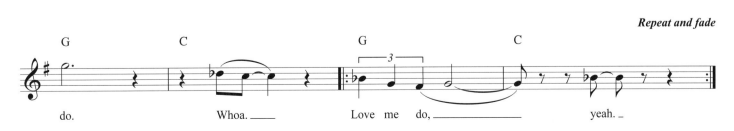

do. _____   Whoa, _____   love __ me   do. _____   Yeah, _____   love   me

Repeat and fade

do.   Whoa. _____   Love   me   do, _____   yeah. __

Me and Bobby McGee

Words and Music by Kris Kristofferson and Fred Foster

Verse
Moderately, in 2

1. Bust-ed flat __ in Bat-on Rouge, wait-in' for a train, __ when I's
2. *See additional lyrics*

feel-in' near __ as fad-ed as __ my __ jeans.

Bob-by thumbed __ a die-sel down __ just be-fore __ it

rained __ that rode us all __ the way to New Or - leans. I

pulled my har-poon __ out of my dirt-y red ban-dan-na. I's

play-in' soft while Bob-by sang the blues, __ yeah. __

Wind-shield wip-ers slap-pin' time, I's __ hold-in' Bob-by's hand in mine.

We sang ev - 'ry song ____ that driv - er knew. ____

Chorus

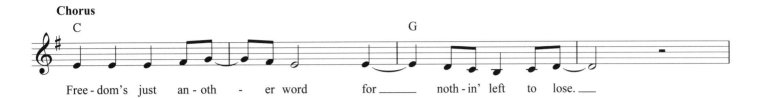

Free - dom's just an - oth - er word for ____ noth - in' left to lose. ____

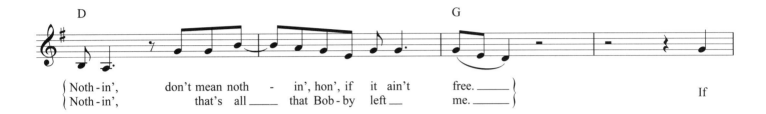

Noth - in', don't mean noth - in', hon', if it ain't free. ____
Noth - in', that's all ____ that Bob - by left ____ me. ____

If

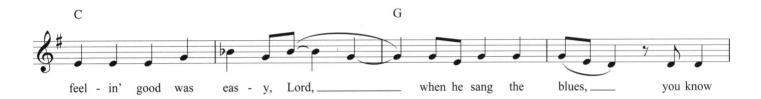

feel - in' good was eas - y, Lord, ____ when he sang the blues, ____ you know

feel - in' good was good e - nough ____ for me, ____

good e - nough ____ for me and my Bob - by Mc - Gee.

Outro

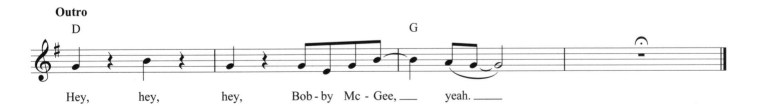

Hey, hey, hey, Bob - by Mc - Gee, ____ yeah. ____

Additional Lyrics

2. From the Kentucky coal mine to the California sun,
Hey, Bobby shared the secrets of my soul.
Through all kinds of weather, through ev'rything we done,
Yeah, Bobby, baby, kept me from the cold.
One day up near Salinas, Lord, I let him slip away.
He's lookin' for that home, and I hope he finds it.
But I'd trade all of my tomorrows for one single yesterday,
To be holdin' Bobby's body next to mine.

Ring of Fire

Words and Music by Merle Kilgore and June Carter

Additional Lyrics

2. The taste of love is sweet
   When hearts like ours meet.
   I feel for you like a child,
   Oh, but the fire went wild.

Stir It Up

Words and Music by Bob Marley

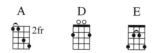

it's o - kay ___ to see what we can do, ba - by. Just _ me and _ you. Come on and

Outro-Chorus

can _ stir your _ pot. So stir it up, ___ lit - tle dar - ling,

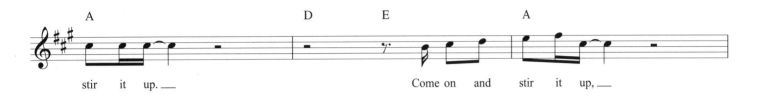

stir it up. ___ Come on and stir it up, ___

Repeat and fade

oo, lit - tle dar - ling, stir it up, ___ yeah,

Additional Lyrics

2. It's time to push the wood, and I'll blaze your fire.
Then I'll satisfy your heart's desire.
Still I stir it together ev'ry minute.
All you got to do, baby, is keep it in and...

3. And then quench me when I'm thirsty.
Come on, cool me down, baby, when I'm hot.
Your recipe, darlin', is so tasty,
And you sure can stir your pot.

Sweet Caroline

Words and Music by Neil Diamond

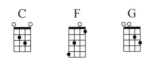

1. Where it be - gan, ___ I can't be - gin to know - in',
   look at the night, ___ and it don't seem so lone - ly. ___

but then I know ___ it's grow - in' strong.
We fill it up ___ with on - ly two.

Was in the spring, ___ and spring be - came the sum - mer.
And when I hurt, ___ hurt - in' runs off my shoul - ders.

Who'd have be - lieved ___ you'd come a - long? ___
How can I hurt ___ when hold - in' you? ___

Pre-Chorus

Hands, ___ touch - in' hands, ___ reach - in' out,
Warm, ___ touch - in' warm, ___

touch - in' me, touch - in' you. ___

Twist and Shout

Words and Music by Bert Russell and Phil Medley

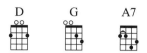

D   G   A7

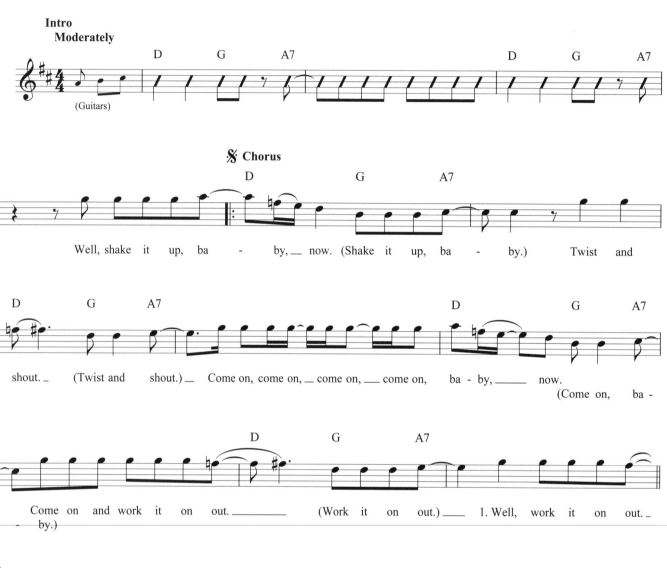

Intro
Moderately

(Guitars)

𝄋 **Chorus**

Well, shake it up, ba - by, __ now. (Shake it up, ba - by.) Twist and

shout. __ (Twist and shout.) __ Come on, come on, __ come on, __ come on, ba - by, _____ now. (Come on, ba -

Come on and work it on out. _____ (Work it on out.) __ 1. Well, work it on out. _
- by.)

Verse

_____ (Work it on out.) __ You know you look so good. _ (Look so good.) _
2., 3. *See additional lyrics*

__ You know you got me go - in' now. (Got me go - in'.) Just like I knew you would. __

__ (Like I knew you would.) __   Well, shake it up, ba- __

Interlude

(Guitars)   Ah.   Ah.   Ah.   Ah.   Ah. __

D.S. al Coda   **Coda**

__ Shake it up, ba-   __ Well, shake it, shake it, shake it, ba-by, now.   (Shake it up, ba-

Well, shake it, shake it, shake it, ba-by, now. (Shake it up, ba - by.) __
-by.)

Ah.   Ah.   Ah.   Ah.   (Guitars)

Additional Lyrics

2., 3. You know you twist, little girl. (Twist, little girl.)
You know you twist so fine. (Twist so fine.)
Come on and twist a little closer now (Twist a little closer.)
And let me know that you're mine. (Let me know you're mine.)

Shake It Off

Words and Music by Taylor Swift, Max Martin and Shellback

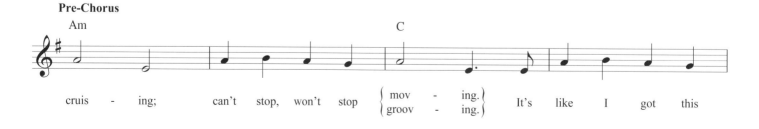

G

shake it off, ___ I shake it off. I, ___ I, I shake it off, ___ I shake it off.

Breakdown

N.C.

Spoken: "Hey, hey, hey! *Just think: while you've been gettin' down and out about the liars and the dirty,*

dirty cheats of the world, you *could've been gettin' down to* *this!* *sick!* *beat!"*

Rap: My ex man brought his new girl-friend, She's like, "Oh my God!" But I'm just gon-na shake. And to the

fel-la o-ver there with the hell-a good hair, won't you come on o-ver, ba-by? We can

D.S. al Coda
(take 2nd ending)

shake, shake, shake. Yeah, _____ oh. _____ 'Cause the

Coda

Outro

Am   C

{ 1. shake } it off, ___ I shake it off. I, ___ I, I shake it off, ___ I shake it
{ 2., 3. Shake }

G

off. I, ___ I, I shake it off, ___ I shake it off. I, ___ I, I

|1., 2.   3.

shake it off, ___ I shake it off.   off.

Hal Leonard Mandolin Play-Along Series

Great Mandolin Publications

from

HAL·LEONARD®

HAL LEONARD MANDOLIN METHOD

INCLUDES TAB

Noted mandolinist and teacher Rich Del Grosso has authored this excellent mandolin method that features great playable tunes in several styles (bluegrass, country, folk, blues) in standard music notation and tablature. The optional audio features play-along duets.

00699296 Book Only $7.99
00695102 Book/Online Audio $15.99

EASY SONGS FOR MANDOLIN

SUPPLEMENTARY SONGBOOK TO
THE HAL LEONARD MANDOLIN METHOD

20 songs to play as you learn mandolin: Annie's Song • California Dreamin' • Let It Be • Puff the Magic Dragon • Scarborough Fair • Where Have All the Flowers Gone? • and more.

00695865 Book Only...................................... $9.99
00695866 Book/CD Pack $15.99

FRETBOARD ROADMAPS – MANDOLIN

INCLUDES TAB

THE ESSENTIAL PATTERNS THAT
ALL THE PROS KNOW AND USE

by Fred Sokolow and Bob Applebaum

The latest installment in our popular Fretboard Roadmaps series is a unique book/CD pack for all mandolin players. The CD includes 48 demonstration tracks for the exercises that will teach players to: play all over the fretboard, in any key; increase their chord, scale and lick vocabulary; play chord-based licks, moveable major and blues scales, first-position major scales and double stops; and more! Includes easy-to-follow diagrams and instructions for all levels of players.

00695357 Book/CD Pack $14.99

MANDOLIN CHORD FINDER

EASY-TO-USE GUIDE TO OVER
1,000 MANDOLIN CHORDS

by Chad Johnson

Learn to play chords on the mandolin with this comprehensive, yet easy-to-use book. The Hal Leonard Mandolin Chord Finder contains over 1,000 chord diagrams for the most important 28 chord types, including three voicings for each chord. Also includes a lesson on chord construction, and a fingerboard chart of the mandolin neck!

00695739 9" X 12" Edition............................. $6.99
00695740 6" X 9" Edition $5.99

MANDOLIN SCALE FINDER

EASY-TO-USE GUIDE TO OVER 1,300 MANDOLIN SCALES

by Chad Johnson

Presents scale diagrams for the most often-used scales and modes in an orderly and easily accessible fashion. Use this book as a reference guide or as the foundation for creating an in-depth practice routine. Includes multiple patterns for each scale, a lesson on scale construction, and a fingerboard chart of the mandolin neck.

00695779 9" X 12" Edition............................. $6.95
00695782 6" X 9" Edition $5.99

BILL MONROE – 16 GEMS

INCLUDES TAB

Authentic mandolin transcriptions of these classics by the Father of Bluegrass: Blue Grass Breakdown • Blue Grass Special • Can't You Hear Me Calling • Goodbye Old Pal • Heavy Traffic Ahead • I'm Going Back to Old Kentucky • It's Mighty Dark to Travel • Kentucky Waltz • Nobody Loves Me • Old Crossroad Is Waitin' • Remember the Cross • Shine Hallelujah Shine • Summertime Is Past and Gone • Sweetheart You Done Me Wrong • Travelin' This Lonesome Road • True Life Blues.

00690310 Mandolin Transcriptions.............. $14.99

O BROTHER, WHERE ART THOU?

INCLUDES TAB

Perfect for beginning to advanced players, this collection contains both note-for-note transcribed mandolin solos, as well as mandolin arrangements of the melody lines for 11 songs from this Grammy-winning Album of the Year: Angel Band • The Big Rock Candy Mountain • Down to the River to Pray • I Am a Man of Constant Sorrow • I Am Weary (Let Me Rest) • I'll Fly Away • In the Highways (I'll Be Somewhere Working for My Lord) • In the Jailhouse Now • Indian War Whoop • Keep on the Sunny Side • You Are My Sunshine. Chord diagrams provided for each song match the chords from the original recording, and all songs are in their original key. Includes tab, lyrics and a mandolin notation legend.

00695762... $15.99

THE ULTIMATE BLUEGRASS MANDOLIN CONSTRUCTION MANUAL

by Roger H. Siminoff

This is the most complete step-by-step treatise ever written on building an acoustical string instrument. Siminoff, a renowned author and luthier, applies over four decades of experience to guide beginners to pros through detailed chapters on wood selection, cutting, carving, shaping, assembly, inlays, fretting, binding and assembly of an F-style mandolin.

00331088... $37.99

Prices, contents and availability are subject to change without notice.

HAL·LEONARD®

Visit Hal Leonard online at www.halleonard.com

Learn To Play Today
with folk music instruction from

Hal Leonard Banjo Method – Second Edition

Authored by Mac Robertson, Robbie Clement & Will Schmid. This innovative method teaches 5-string, bluegrass style. The method consists of two instruction books and two cross-referenced supplement books that offer the beginner a carefully-paced and interest-keeping approach to the bluegrass style.

Method Book 1
00699500 Book $7.99
00695101 Book/Online Audio $16.99

Method Book 2
00699502...$7.99

Supplementary Songbooks
00699515 Easy Banjo Solos $9.99
00699516 More Easy Banjo Solos $9.99

Hal Leonard Dulcimer Method – Second Edition

by Neal Hellman

A beginning method for the Appalachian dulcimer with a unique new approach to solo melody and chord playing. Includes tuning, modes and many beautiful folk songs all demonstrated on the audio accompaniment. Music and tablature.
00699289 Book $9.99
00697230 Book/Online Audio $16.99

The Hal Leonard Complete Harmonica Method – Chromatic Harmonica

by Bobby Joe Holman

The only harmonica method to present the chromatic harmonica in 14 scales and modes in all 12 keys!
00841286 Book/Online Audio..............................$12.99

The Hal Leonard Complete Harmonica Method – The Diatonic Harmonica

by Bobby Joe Holman

This terrific method book/CD pack specific to the diatonic harmonica covers all six positions! It contains more than 20 songs and musical examples.
00841285 Book/Online Audio..............................$12.99

Hal Leonard Fiddle Method

by Chris Wagoner

The Hal Leonard Fiddle Method is the perfect introduction to playing folk, bluegrass and country styles on the violin. Many traditional tunes are included to illustrate a variety of techniques. The accompanying audio includes many tracks for demonstration and play-along. Covers: instrument selection and care; playing positions; theory; slides & slurs; shuffle feel; bowing; drones; playing "backup"; cross-tuning; and much more!
00311415 Book $6.99
00311416 Book/Online Audio $10.99

The Hal Leonard Mandolin Method – Second Edition

Noted mandolinist and teacher Rich Del Grosso has authored this excellent mandolin method that features great playable tunes in several styles (bluegrass, country, folk, blues) in standard music notation and tablature. The audio features play-along duets.
00699296 Book $7.99
00695102 Book/Online Audio $15.99

Hal Leonard Oud Method

by John Bilezikjian

This book teaches the fundamentals of standard Western music notation in the context of oud playing. It also covers: types of ouds, tuning the oud, playing position, how to string the oud, scales, chords, arpeggios, tremolo technique, studies and exercises, songs and rhythms from Armenia and the Middle East, and 25 audio tracks for demonstration and play along.
00695836 Book/Online Audio..............................$12.99

Hal Leonard Ukulele Method Book 1

INCLUDES TAB

by Lil' Rev

This comprehensive and easy-to-use beginner's guide by acclaimed performer and uke master Lil' Rev includes many fun songs of different styles to learn and play. Includes: types of ukuleles, tuning, music reading, melody playing, chords, strumming, scales, tremolo, music notation and tablature, a variety of music styles, ukulele history and much more.
00695847 Book $6.99
00695832 Book/Online Audio $10.99

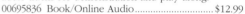

Visit Hal Leonard Online at
www.halleonard.com